Look and Find®

Disney

PLANES
FIRE & RESCUE

pi kids® phoenix international publications, inc.

Propwash Junction needs one more firefighter before reopening its airport and hosting the annual Corn Festival. Dusty Crophopper is on his way to get certified as a firefighting vehicle! Look for Dusty's friends who are counting on him:

Sparky

Skipper

Leadbottom

Mayday

Dottie

Chug

At the Piston Peak National Park, Blade Ranger will train Dusty to fight fires. But first, Dusty meets the crew of Piston Peak Air Attack. Can you find Dusty's new friends?

Dynamite

Dipper

Avalanche

Drip

Pinecone

Blackout

Windlifter

Blade coaches Dusty to fly low through Augerin Canyon. Flying low is Dusty's specialty! Blade is impressed with how well Dusty maneuvers through the course. Look for these obstacles that Dusty needs to dodge:

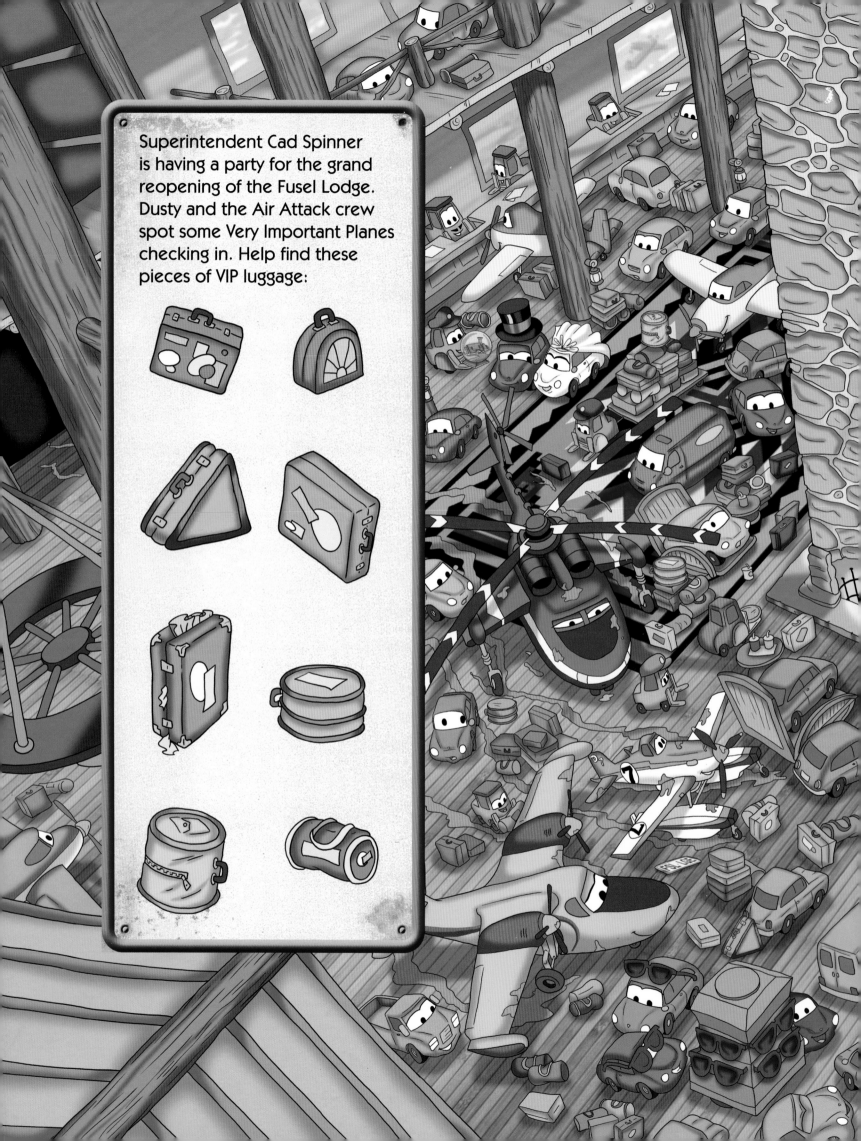

Superintendent Cad Spinner is having a party for the grand reopening of the Fusel Lodge. Dusty and the Air Attack crew spot some Very Important Planes checking in. Help find these pieces of VIP luggage:

Oh no! A wildfire is traveling across the park. While Dusty and the Air Attack crew douse the flames with retardant, look for these things in the fire's path:

To protect the guests, Blade orders an evacuation. Ol' Jammer and Pulaski help the campers get out safely. Stay calm and help locate these guests:

Dusty is a hero! He helped put out the fire—but he got injured along the way. Maru will fix him up, better than new! Look around Maru's shop for these spare parts:

panel

tire

yoke

piston

spark plug

muffler

propeller

spring

Everyone back in Propwash Junction is proud of Dusty for becoming a firefighter. The airport has reopened, and the Corn Festival is in full swing! See if you can find these corny items:

cotton corndy

topiary

hat

collector mug

corncob on a stick

balloon

sunglasses

Even though Dusty is taking a break from racing, he's still a champion! Zoom back to Propwash Junction and find this racing memorabilia:

trophy

bumper sticker

mug

magazine

plaque

poster

All sorts of vehicles enjoy Piston Peak National Park. Look for these camping supplies around the grounds:

cooler

thermos

rope

this tent

tire-shaped bag

ax

As Dusty flies low through the canyon, he sees the park's wildlife up close. Can you fly back and find these forest dwellers?

Don't forget to visit the gift shop during your stay at the Fusel Lodge! Can you find these souvenirs?

mug

keychain

license plate

hat

snow globe

postcard

As the Air Attack crew works on the wildfire, locate these plumes of smoke:

Safety is Blade's primary concern. Return to the evacuation and look for letters that spell:

S-A-F-E-T-Y

Hang out with Dusty and see if you can find these posters in Maru's service hangar:

Propwash Junction celebrates corn because so many different things are made with it. Head back to the Corn Festival and find these corn-based products:

toothpaste

Vita-Minamulch

paint

crayons

battery

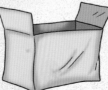
cardboard box

bottle of glue